MW00417246

THE
RICHEST MAN IN BABYLON FOR TODAY

New Secrets for Building Wealth in the 21st Century

FRED SIEGEL

author of *Investing for Cowards* and
401(k)s for Cowards

with RICK CRANDALL

Grammaton Press
New Orleans

Grammaton Press, LLC
601 Poydras Street, Suite 2650
New Orleans, LA 70130
(504) 566-3619
books@grammatonpress.com

As noted in the book, the website for this book welcomes your questions and has additional material:
www.TheRichestManInBabylon.com

STANDARD DISCLAIMER

This publication is designed to provide accurate information in regard to the subject matter covered. It is sold with the understanding that this book is not designed to render legal, accounting, investment, or other professional service. If investment or financial advice or other expert assistance is required, the services of a competent professional should be sought.

From a Declaration of Principles jointly adopted by a Committee of the American Bar Association and a Committee of Publishers.

The Richest Man in Babylon for Today
/ Fred Siegel with Rick Crandall

Printed in Korea

ISBN 0-9679366-3-2
10 9 8 7 6 5 4 3 2 1

What people are saying about
The Richest Man in Babylon for Today...

"*The Richest Man in Babylon for Today* should be included in every 'personal success' library. It provides the steps needed to achieve individual fulfillment and financial independence"
— Somers White, CMC, CSP, CPAE,
President, The Somers White Company, Inc.

"*The Richest Man in Babylon for Today* is an updated, ready-to-go, reality-check guide to financial success in the 21st century. This new rendering of this timeless classic offers universal truths in user-friendly parlance and underscores a surefire formula for success."
— Louise Underdahl, PhD,
author, *The Soul of Work*

"A splendid read! The author deserves a lot more than a pat on the back for this brilliant rewriting of *The Richest Man in Babylon.* While reading the original earlier this year, I was impressed by its timeliness. When I read *The Richest Man in Babylon for Today,* I was even more impressed. The author has maintained the integrity and enlightenment of the original while shining the bright light of the 21st century upon them. Now, the book is both timeless and timely."
— Jay Conrad Levinson
author, *Guerrilla Marketing* series of books

"Superb! This one has all the markings of a future success classic! I'm a big fan of the original *The Richest Man In Babylon*. I absolutely loved the new book. It is written in an easily digestible and enjoyable style. The examples presented are solid ideas that at the same can help the reader develop a deeper understanding of what it takes to develop wealth.

— Josh Hinds, co-author, *One Question to Success*
http://GetMotivation.com

"An elegantly simple guide to growing personal wealth that is motivating and easy to read. *The Richest Man in Babylon For Today* reminds us that we are the ones responsible for our financial destiny."

— Dee Hansford,
author, *The Magic of Employee Recognition*

"Once I began to read, I could not stop. With examples you can relate to and almost feel, the author has made the book a rare and valuable combination of information, inspiration, enlightenment, and entertainment."

— Henry Ford, author, *Success is YOU!*

Acknowledgments

They say, "No man is an island." I say that especially applies to authors of books. This book, *The Richest Man in Babylon for Today,* is a product of combined efforts and patient encouragement.

The primary assistance came from Rick Crandall, my editor and cohort in recreating and updating this compelling story. He became as excited about the project as I did, which helped greatly to move it along. I appreciate his research and care in "babying" the book to its current form. I also appreciate his well placed "nags" as deadlines approached. Rick is an author in his own right, having written a number of books on marketing "for people who hate to sell." He can be reached at RickCrandall.com.

Carolynn Crandall of Select Press deserves kudos for her page design and typesetting. She always makes a book easier to read because of its physical appearance. I also welcomed her many suggestions on general grammatical style.

Appreciation goes to members of The Siegel Group, Inc., my Director of Operations, Tanya

Dejean-Curtis, my Executive Assistant, Katrice Harris and my partner Wayne Traina for their encouragement and assistance as I worked on the manuscript.

Thanks to Karla Martinez, Executive Director of Grammaton Press, LLC and Myra Martinez, CFO of Fred Siegel International, Inc., for taking care of the many details to publish.

Nadia Martinez, Executive Director of Fred Siegel International, Inc. helped me remain organized and focused on the work. She developed the book's new website and its new Ezine while making sure I was prepared for all interviews and public appearances along the way.

George Foster continues to impress me with his excellent book cover designs.

I thank Phil Hoover, General Manager and Market Manager of Entercom Radio in New Orleans for his friendship, guidance, and foresight in using the dynamics of radio as a means of helping people achieve their financial goals.

Special thanks go to the "beautiful Ms. Elaine," my wife and best friend since 1970. She always makes me feel I can accomplish anything I want and, indeed, I consider my greatest accomplishment to be attracting and holding on to such an excellent companion. When she's around I feel like I am "The Richest Man in Babylon."

Contents

DEDICATION

To all of my listeners, viewers,
readers and clients...
for your confidence, trust, and
loyal support over the years.

Introduction

The little book *The Richest Man in Babylon* by George S. Clason has been called a "timeless classic," and "the most inspiring book on wealth ever written." Millions of copies have been sold.

While the original book has some great ideas for financial success, it is unfortunately disjointed, redundant, and out of date for the 21st century. Few people know that the reason is because it was originally written as a series of separate stories, starting in 1926. These were published in various forms, a few stories at a time. Many were given away as booklets by financial institutions and insurance agents.

Even fewer people know that nine of the ten stories, plus some extra material, were published as the book *Gold Ahead.* This was in 1937, the same year *Think and Grow Rich* was first published. However, *Gold Ahead* didn't enjoy great popularity until it was retitled *The Richest Man in Babylon* in 1955.

When I've talked with people about the original *Richest Man in Babylon*, they've remembered it fondly for its inspiration. However, few read past the first couple of chapters because the language and setting of ancient Babylon is more distracting than helpful in today's times. And the only advice the book provides on how to invest your money is to become a money lender.

These criticisms aside, I loved the original book and rewrote it to make its valuable principles more relevant for the world we live in today. Some of the principles—like saving 10 percent before you spend any money—can be the foundation of your future wealth.

Of course, there is no Babylon anymore. This modern version of the classic story takes place in the United States. In some ways, the US is the modern "Babylon"—a wonder of the world protected for years by its "walls" of oceans. Just as in the ancient case, many are jealous of Babylon's power and wealth, and they attack it.

The point of this book is to teach the basics of how to get ahead financially. In making the book more relevant to our modern age, I have changed the stories to a modern setting, eliminated redundancy, and updated the older principles and added new ones that apply to your situation now.

I welcome your questions and stories of success. Please share them with me at the book's website. There, you'll also find additional material on investing and stocks (please go to www.TheRichestManInBabylonForToday.com).

An Historical Note

The site of ancient Babylon is in modern day Iraq, by the Euphrates River. The Hanging Gardens of Babylon was one of the Seven Wonders of the Ancient World. The Tower of Babel had also been built there.

Because it was in a river valley, Babylon had fertile soil. However, the riches of Babylon were created through man's efforts to develop available resources. Their extensive use of irrigation for farming (and for the hanging gardens) was a master feat of engineering. Trade naturally followed. Today, Babylon is gone. Without human industry, the site has reverted back to its natural state.

Ancient scholars wrote about Babylon as a legendary center of wealth. This is why it was picked as the site of the financial parables in the original book. Babylon may even have invented money as we know it. Before that time, all purchasing and selling involved barter (thus the word "trade" for business).

I've found the lessons from the original book to be invaluable in my life. With this rewritten book, I have a chance to pass on to you both the old lessons and a few new ones for today. I hope you enjoy them as much as I do.

– Fred Siegel
New Orleans

THE RICHEST MAN IN BABYLON FOR TODAY

1

You Must *Want* to Be Better Off

It is part of the cure to wish to be cured.

SENECA

John and Mary were discouraged about their financial situation—and for good reason. They had been married for seven years and had two children. John worked at a factory and Mary worked at a law office. Both made reasonable salaries, but they had little to show for their efforts.

They made enough to pay most bills, but were behind on their credit cards. They went to the lake for a week each summer. They had occasional nights out, but often they were too tired to go out. Renting movies and buying pizza was about it.

Are you running hard but getting nowhere?

It was starting to look as if nothing would ever change. John and

1

> *Too many hardworking people have little to show for it.*

Mary felt a bit like hamsters running in a wheel. They kept running but didn't get anywhere. This is the situation of many average hardworking people. They make payments for their housing, for their cars, for health insurance, life insurance, credit cards, and more. They work hard but have little to look forward to. This is a problem in all countries.

John and Mary *wanted* to get ahead, but they didn't know how to direct their efforts.

> *Free enterprise is uneven.*

On a philosophical level, this type of situation is a problem for the capitalist system. Despite an unequal distribution of wealth, however, the capitalist system has proved to be better than any alternative. Some people, like Bill Gates, make more money than anybody could spend. Others, like John and Mary, make less than they need to live full lives. Fortunately, you can attain financial success without inventing the "next great thing."

Back to John and Mary

When they had too much *month* left at the end of the money, John and Mary would stretch out paying bills and would use their credit cards for groceries and gas. Nobody went hungry, and they had a big-screen TV, a high-speed Internet connection, two cars, and a nice stereo. They weren't bad off, but there was always money pressure.

How do you learn about money?

John was a traditional guy and felt responsible for doing something about their financial situation. But he didn't know what to do. He was a good worker but wasn't likely to start his own business. He might be able to get an extra part-time job, but it wouldn't pay that much. Mary was willing to do her part by working and taking care of the house, but she didn't know anything about handling money either. And she'd like to spend more time at home while the kids were still young.

John and Mary didn't have to go far to see people like themselves, struggling to make ends meet, in the neighboring tract houses. In fact, complaints about money were common at the bowling alley and the local restaurants where they occasionally went with their friends.

Enter Roberto

It was the next day after work, when John was having a beer with Roberto, that the topic of money came up again.

Roberto said, "You know, John, we're always complaining about not having enough money, but when are we going to *do* something about it?"

"What do you expect me to do?" asked John. "Those ads on the Internet are scams, and I don't want to start selling vitamins or some other product to my friends. Sure, some people make money that way, but that's not for me."

If We're So Smart, Why Aren't We Rich?

"The closest I've come to big money was in a dream," said John. "In the dream, I had money in the bank and could afford to take my wife out to fancy restaurants whenever it was my turn to cook. We took a cruise to Europe and traveled around to fancy places for a month. The kids were taken care of by our live-in help. I went to society charity parties and gave my church enough for the new addition. We were as happy as newlyweds."

"So why are you so grumpy? In fact, I could use a dream like that myself. I'm so far down, I don't even *dream* rich anymore," said Roberto.

Disappointment can motivate you to change.

"I'm grumpy because when I woke up, I felt even poorer by contrast. It's time we did something about money. We've known each other since we were kids. We played on the team together in high school. We drink together. We work together. We're as smart as most of the people we know and smarter than a lot of them."

Act on Your Desire to Succeed

"We've put in the hours and have been good workers," said John. "We make decent salaries. We live in the richest country in the world, yet we have nothing to show for it. We're almost middle-

*Dreams are a dime a dozen . . .
it's their execution that counts.*

THEODORE ROOSEVELT

aged and don't have $100 in our pockets to splurge with!"

"I agree, John, but I don't like to be reminded of it. I don't see my kids much since the divorce, but I worry about them. Not only would I like them to be able to go to college, I'd like them to do better than we have. But I don't see what good talking about it does."

"I've avoided thinking about it too. But enough's enough. I've drifted for too long!"

"Look John, I know the feeling. In the back of my mind, maybe I figured that good people get their rewards. Of course, I of all people am not particularly virtuous, but I guess I was hoping that something would happen *to* me. Like maybe you'd win the lottery and share it with me!"

Try Something New

"You know, Roberto," said John, "we've never talked about this. Maybe we can encourage each other to do something different. You know that old saying, 'If you keep doing what you've always done, you'll keep getting what you've always got.'"

> **If you keep doing what you've always done, you'll keep getting what you've always got.**

"Well," said Roberto, "the way I heard it was that Einstein said the definition of insanity is *doing the same thing over and over and expecting a new result.*"

"Same thing. The point is that we need to try something different if we want things to be better."

"John, sometimes I feel a little guilty about the idea of making money. My mother's relatives were all in unions and they used to say that any rich guy was a crook."

"I know the feeling," said John. "And some

> **It's okay to make money.**

of those guys *are* crooks, paying themselves big salaries even when their companies lose money, while they're asking for job and salary cuts from the workers. Look at all the bankrupt companies and CEOs who had 'golden parachutes' in the last few years.

"Maybe the first thing we need to do is decide it's all right to have more money. That's one way we can help each other. And another way would be to spend more time with people who *have* money. We only hang out with guys like us who never get ahead."

"You know, John, I just saw Bob Kozlowski. He's the one guy from our neighborhood who's made it big. He has his own company and he's a friendly guy. Why don't we ask his advice?"

"Great idea, Roberto. He's supposed to be the richest guy in town. He's even on some government economic advisory panel. We need a new approach. Maybe he can help us if he has the time."

"I wonder if the reason we've never had any money is that we've never really *tried* to get it.

Many people think that for one person to get rich, another has to be poor (a "zero-sum game"). That's not true. The more productive we all are, the more there is available for us all to share. The stock market is an example. Stocks can keep going up as the companies produce more and make more money. No one has to lose money over the long term.

Find skilled advisers. We've succeeded at our jobs because we wanted to. Maybe we can succeed with money by focusing on it. And asking for advice from people who have already succeeded is a good start. Let's make an appointment with Bob."

> *The secret of getting ahead is just getting started.*
>
> **MARK TWAIN**

2

The Richest Man in "Babylon"

*When the student is ready,
the master appears.*

BUDDHIST PROVERB

*B*ob Kozlowski was rich. So rich that he couldn't spend his money as fast as it came in. His place in *Forbes 400 Richest Americans* was a given.

When his boyhood friends came to him for advice, he was happy to talk with them. John started by asking Bob how he had done so much better than everyone else when they'd all started in the same neighborhood and all worked hard.

"Of course, I had some luck. But my first four businesses didn't make any money. I kept trying, and I learned as I went along. If you're still scraping by, it's because either you haven't learned the laws of money, or you haven't applied them."

Improve yourself by other men's writings
so that you shall come easily by what others
have labored hard for.

SENECA

First, Appreciate the Value of Money

"First you have to *care* about money. Not for its own sake, but because it represents personal freedom and the ability to accomplish things. Money multiplies the value of life. It allows you to travel, learn, and help others much more than you could without it.

"When I realized this, I knew that all I had to work with was time and knowledge. Since I wasn't particularly knowledgeable and had no advantages over anyone else in the neighborhood, I decided I had better learn more.

LAWS OF
MONEY

1. CARE
2. SAVE 10%
3. INVEST

Educate yourself.

"I started to study wealth. I read the old classics *Think and Grow Rich*, *Acres of Diamonds*, and *The Richest Man in Babylon*. They were all good and inspirational, but most were written a long time ago.

"Other books focused largely on positive thinking, books like *I Can* and *Success Through a Positive Mental Attitude*. It is clear from modern

*Luck? I don't know anything about luck.
I've never banked on it, and I'm afraid of
people who do. Luck to me is
something else: hard work—and realizing
what is opportunity and what isn't.*

LUCILLE BALL

research on self-esteem and optimism that a positive attitude helps you. However, too much of the early work bordered on the mysterious.

"There are no magic paths to riches. You are going to have to work hard until your money starts working for you."

Classic Success Stories

"The old Horatio Alger stories are cited as the classic American stories of 'poor boy gets rich through hard work and honest character.' I've actually read some of them. In the basic plot, the poor but honest boy *does* work hard. But he also finds a rich man's wallet and returns it. Then the rich man gives him a job and helps him. Even in the original *The Richest Man in Babylon*, the wealthy narrator giving advice had been taken on by a rich man and later made an heir.

It's up to you.

"In today's world, you'll be better off counting on your own efforts. Either you have to take bigger risks and start your own business like I did, or you have to make yourself more valuable to those you work for, and then manage your money for the long term.

Shallow men believe in luck.
Strong men believe in cause and effect.

RALPH WALDO EMERSON

| **You get what you give.** | "I like Zig Zigler's famous saying that you can get anything you want if you *first* help other people get what *they* want." |

Roberto broke in: "You know, Bob, sometimes I think that I *deserve* more than I get. Other people who aren't as smart or honest as I am have gotten rich. But what you're saying is that I need to *take responsibility* for my own success."

Lesson 1: Pay Yourself First—Save Money

"That's a good point about responsibility," said Bob. "But here is what started me on my path to financial independence: I decided that *a part of all I earned was mine to keep.*"

"But *everything* I earn belongs to me, doesn't it?" said Roberto.

"Not really," Bob replied. "Most of what you earn is already committed to your expenses—your house, food, car insurance, and so on. You're the only one you don't pay. In fact, tell me how much you have left from last year's earnings."

"Nothing!" said Roberto and John together.

> **A part of all you earn is yours to keep. This may not sound like much, but it is what you need to save money.**

"*Pay yourself first,* before you spend any money. You may have to put off a few optional purchases like the latest clothing or eating out, but you won't miss the money after the habit is established.

"When I started studying money, I realized that every dollar I spent today could be $10 in a few years if I invested it. This made me much more careful about wasting a few dollars here and a few there because they didn't matter.

"Wealth is like a tree—it grows from tiny seeds. As the Chinese say, '*The best time to plant your tree was 20 years ago. The next best time is today.*' The sooner you plant those wealth seeds, the sooner they'll grow."

The Problems of Sudden Wealth

"Interestingly enough, the fact that it takes time to build wealth is to your advantage. Most of the people who suddenly inherit money, or win the lottery, end up wasting their money.

"When you have a stream of income and are used to living within your means, you are much more likely to appreciate money *and* keep it."

A Lesson Applied, a Habit Started

John's wife, Mary, agreed to commit to saving money. They had automatic payroll deductions taken from their checks. Roberto opened a separate bank account for his savings.

Strangely enough, they didn't really miss the money. In fact, it seemed to make little difference in their lifestyles. Once in a while they were tempted to buy a new TV or something they saw in the stores, but they didn't.

At the end of a year, Bob sent the men a note inviting them to meet him at a local restaurant and report on their financial progress.

"Well," said Bob, "have you paid yourselves at least 10 percent of what you made this year?"

"I have," said Roberto.

John said, "We saved our 10 percent, but then the car's transmission broke. We spent some of our savings on repairs. So we ended up with only half of what we had saved."

Earn Money From Your Savings

"And what did you do with the money you saved?" asked Bob.

"I left mine in a separate bank account," said Roberto.

"If you remember the story of the 'talents' from the Bible," Bob said, "you know that the person who was given money and buried it to keep it safe made the wrong choice. If everyone sat on their money, the economy would stagnate. You made a good start by saving the money, but you need to help your money grow."

"But you never said anything about investing the money," said Roberto.

"That's the lesson for today. And John, what did you and Mary do with your savings?"

Don't Take Advice From Amateurs

"Well," said John, " a guy at work had a hot tip on a stock. His brother-in-law knew a guy

who knew a company with a new product coming out. So I bought shares with the money we had left after we fixed the car. Unfortunately, the stock is down, so our money is tied up and we've lost a lot of it."

"It makes no sense to use a guy who works with you for advice on stocks," said Bob. "While once in a while a tip is right, most such tips are wrong, or they are spread by people who are *selling* their shares. You've killed your wealth-tree, John, so you'll need to start over."

Lesson 2: Put Your Money to Work

"Your money should work for you," said Bob. "But you either need to obtain advice from people who really know what they're doing, or invest in things you're familiar with.

"A couple of famous investors, Warren Buffett and Peter Lynch, essentially said that you should invest in companies you understand. For instance, Wal-Mart was a favorite investment of both of them because they could see why it was successful. You might invest in a new fast-food franchise if you see a local one is thriving. Or you can invest in a part-time business where you can control your own efforts.

| **Stock market limitations.** | "Unless you enjoy follow- ing stocks using a service like *Value Line* that has a proven sys- tem for rating stocks, you're best |

off in an index fund. This buys the overall market for you, so you share in the general business pros- perity in this country. It will go up and down, but over the long term, it has always gone up."*

"If you decide to invest in bonds, use the US Treasury's I-bonds. They protect you from infla- tion and pay a small interest rate over that. They're absolutely safe."

The Next Year: Money Making Money

The next year, John reported, "Mary and I found the habit of saving much easier this year. We actually saved a little over 10 percent, so we had a small emergency fund for things like car repairs.

"We did something unusual with our money. Mary has always collected little figurines from thrift stores and garage sales. This year, she started buying some just to resell on eBay.

---

* For much more on successful stock market strategies, see my book *Investing for Cowards* (reference on page 137).

"We never thought of our-
selves as wanting to be in busi-
ness," continued John, "but
we've sold about 80 percent of
what we've offered on eBay
and made a good profit. Mary
now has friends among collectors all over the
country. We've made almost 100 percent on our
money and have some inventory as well. And we
now have a shared hobby."

Roberto invests well.

"I've also saved over 10
percent," said Roberto. "I invested it with a friend who owns
an upholstery business. He buys
fabric for each job as he sells it. He makes 100
percent profit on the fabric. But once in a while
he can buy close-out fabric for ten cents on the

dollar. And there are other
supplies that he can get for
about half off if he buys a
truckload at a time. I've put
up the money for some bulk
buying like this, and he pays
me as he does each job. We
split his savings so I've made about 25 percent
on the money I've invested with him."

"That's great," said Bob. "Now, what have you done with the profits on your money?"

"We always seem to be able to buy more figurines," said John, "so I guess all our profits are in inventory—and that builds our business."

"I took an extra vacation this winter to Club Med," said Roberto.

Using profits well. "John and Mary invested their profits, which then can make more money for them. But Roberto didn't.

"Roberto 'ate the children' of his savings. If you spend your profits, how do you expect them to work for you? The compounding value of money earning money, which then earns more money, and so forth, really pays off over time. In fact, Einstein is variously credited with calling compounding the eighth wonder of the world or the most powerful force in the universe. Right now, you should be investing, not spending. When you have a substantial stake, *then* you can enjoy some of your profits."

On Their Way

The following year, Bob got together with Roberto and John again. "How's it going, guys?" asked Bob.

"We're doing well," said John. "We've invested in an index fund for extra retirement money, and we still make money selling online."

"Great," said Bob. "You've learned three lessons well: First, to live on less than you earn. Second, to take advice only from people who know what they're doing. And third, to make your money work for you.

1) **Live on less than you earn.**

2) **Take advice only from experts.**

3) **Make your money work for you.**

"You now know how to acquire money, keep it, and use it. In addition to being better off, you have learned self-discipline and long-term planning, so you are now also qualified for more responsible jobs. If you don't find one in your own company, or another business, talk to me about working in my company.

"How about you, Roberto?"

"I've saved money. I invested most of it in a house that came on the market that was a real bargain. My payments are not much more than I was paying for rent. And there are tax breaks. I also got remarried—to an old friend who came back into town. Between us, we save even more.

"I still invest in my friend's business occasionally," continued Roberto, "but most of my money goes into the house or extra mortgage payments. The house is going up at more than inflation, so now I have a serious net worth."

"Wonderful, Roberto. The same offer goes for you. If you don't find the responsibility you now qualify for at your work, look me up. We can always find a place for someone who has demonstrated self-discipline and initiative."

A part of all you earn is yours to keep.

3

Seven Ways to Have More Money

The way to wealth is plain: industry and frugality.
BENJAMIN FRANKLIN

*T*he pattern of boom and bust has occurred many times throughout economic history. The cycle ending with the stock market Crash of 1929 is the best known.

A more recent boom-and-bust cycle was Silicon Valley in California. New high-tech companies sold stock for outrageous prices. When the bubble burst, there were massive layoffs and company closures.

How Can You Fix an Economy?

Several wise mayors in Silicon Valley got together and discussed what they could do to return to prosperity. They consulted with noted economists. But the old saying—that if you put all the economists end to end, they couldn't reach a conclusion—turned out to be true!

The combination of factors that produces a successful economy is very complicated and is still not well understood. Sometimes the government can help by creating programs to employ people. Other times, when governments cut taxes, people spend more money and tax revenues *increase*.

After endless hours of consultation, discussion, posturing, and debate, the mayors knew no more than when they started.

Why not just take from the rich?

The mayor of one town said, "Some people seem to know how to make money no matter what the economy is like. If we raised taxes on the rich, we could get more money from them without hurting the poor who make up the majority of voters."

"That would be like killing the goose that laid the golden eggs," said Mayor Pat Chin. "The people who create jobs and generate tax revenue could either leave or cut back hiring if we taxed them more.

"Instead, we should teach everyone how to make money; then everyone will be prosperous,

Can money success be taught?

and there will be more money from taxes."

Jolene, another mayor, said, "*We* can't teach people how to make money. Most politicians who make money in office do so by using their influence in crooked ways.

"Government doesn't produce anything," continued Jolene. "We rely on business people to produce goods and services. Let's ask *them* how to teach people to handle their money better."

Will the rich want to share the wealth?

"Why would people with money want to help other people make money?" asked Pat.

"I believe I can answer that," said Leroy Brown, who until now had been quiet. "I didn't go into politics until I retired from my business. I made quite a lot of money and felt it was time to give back to the community.

"Too many people believe that if one person gets rich the money is taken from other people. In fact, everyone can be prosperous. Let's take the simplest example. If there are two of us in an economy and I produce more corn and you produce more chickens, we can trade and both have more than we had the year before. As long as people are productive, there's more for everyone."

Money Means Service

"People make money when they provide things that other people want," Leroy continued. "If everyone made more money, there would be more goods and services for all of us.

"There is always money in an economy, but sometimes people are too worried to spend. And when they cut back their buying, there is less income for those who sell to them.

"Rich people *want* other people to have money. More money in the economy means people are producing more goods and services the rich want, and it also means that others have the money to purchase more from the rich."

To Get Answers About Wealth, Ask Someone With Money!

"Fine, if the rich are willing to be so helpful, let's ask them to teach people how to do better," said Jolene. "Who's the richest man in the area?"

"I believe that would be Bob Kozlowski," said an adviser. "He has a huge company and is on the governor's economic advisory commission. He's also a big contributor to charity."

———
Bob comes through.
———

The mayors made an appointment with Bob, and he appeared in front of the group a few days later. "Thank you for coming, Mr. Kozlowski," said Jolene.

"Happy to be here, and call me Bob."

"As my assistant told you when he scheduled this meeting, we're looking for ways to help everyday people become financially successful."

"That's a worthwhile goal," said Bob. "The more people who have an economic stake in this area, the stronger the economy, and the better off we'll all be."

You *Can* Teach People How to Have More Money

"Bob," said one of the mayors, "the economy in our area is down. With fewer people working, tax revenues are down, and that makes it difficult to deliver the necessary services. A few people like yourself seem to know how to make and keep money, but most citizens are in

*Surplus wealth is a sacred trust which
its possessor is bound to administer in his
lifetime for the good of the community.*

ANDREW CARNEGIE

debt and don't hang on to any of the money they make."

"We'd like this area to be prosperous," said Jolene. "We hoped you could tell us if there's a secret to making money and if it can be taught."

"What I know about money can easily be taught to others," responded Bob. "I'd be happy to teach a group of people. Then they can teach the secrets of making money to others. In fact, I've boiled it down to seven simple principles."

THE SEVEN LAWS OF MONEY

A few weeks later, Bob's first class on money began. "As most of you know, I'm Bob Kozlowski. I started out poor from a working-class family, but I really wanted to be rich."

Law #1

Save 10 Percent to Create a Stake

"There are hundreds of ways to make money. You can work for many different types of companies or government agencies. You can manufacture something. You can farm. You can provide a service. The possibilities are endless.

> **Law #1:**
>
> **To start on the path to wealth, first put aside 10% of your income every month.**

"But, no matter how you earn money, pay yourself first. A simple guide is to put aside 10 percent of your income *before* you start spending.

"Of course, saving 10 percent takes discipline. The nice thing is that, as it gets to be a habit, you don't really miss the money you're saving. And soon you will feel proud of your saving 10 percent every month. In contrast, you'll hardly remember what you spent the other 90 percent on."

Law #2

Budget to Control Your Spending

"Law 2 relates to Law 1," continued Bob. "Some people say, 'I can't get by on what I make now. How can I save 10 percent off the top?' Let's take all of you as an example. You are all having trouble making ends meet, yet you don't all make the same amount of money. Some of you support large families. Some of you make half the money of others.

"You may have heard of Parkinson's Law which says work expands to fill the available time. Well, spending expands to use the money available!

Desires are infinite.

"Everyone has more things they'd like to buy than they have money to spend on them. And no matter how much you spend, you'll still have unfulfilled desires waiting for the next money available!

Law #2: Control your expenses with a budget.

"Create a budget for what you really have to spend every month," advised Bob. "You don't really have to have new clothes most months. You don't have to subscribe to cable TV. You don't have to eat out. You'll have room in your budget for some of these expenses, but don't let them just happen.

"There is an interesting phenomenon with budgeting. If you keep a diary of *every penny* you spend for a month, two things will happen. First, you'll tend to cut back on the little expenses, like buying a soft drink or a snack, because it's too much trouble to write them down. Second, you'll see how much a daily cup of coffee or a

Budgeting means control.

The budget should be balanced.

CICERO

pack of cigarettes adds up to each month. You'll see how you can save money just by changing some of your habits."

At this point, one of the students in the audience raised his hand and said, "What's the point of living if you have to scrimp on everything? I think it's my right to enjoy the good things in life. A budget would turn me into a slave or a robot. It would drain all the pleasure out of life."

"I understand how you feel," said Bob. "But unplanned spending got you to where you are today. A man without money is *already* a slave in some ways: a slave to his job or to his creditors.

Budget	
House	$1,200
Food	$400
Utilities	$150
Car	$300
Health insurance	$200
Mad money	$75
Other	?

"You're the one who sets your budget. *Your budget can become your slave.* It can protect you from the temptation to waste money on low priorities. And you can include some 'mad money' in your budget to indulge yourself occasionally.

"You must decide if you want to spend every dollar pursuing short-term pleasures—or have long-term financial independence."

I am indeed rich, since my income
is superior to my expense,
and my expense is equal to my wishes.
EDWARD GIBBON

38   *THE RICHEST MAN IN BABYLON FOR TODAY*

Make Your Money Work for You

Law
#3

"Having your money work for you is how you build your fortune," said Bob.

"If your money sits in the bank or in a CD, it can pay you anywhere from 1 percent to 10 percent a year, depending on the prevailing interest rate and other factors. While bank accounts and CDs are safe and guaranteed by the government, they will always define the *lowest* return you can safely receive on your money.

"Your true wealth is not in the money you earn. It is in making your money work *for* you— the income you create that comes in whether you work or not. This is called *compounding*—when the return on your money earns more money.

"For long-term investments like 401(k)s or other retirement plans, the stock market is the way to go. Historically, it has returned over 10 percent a year. It has a lot of ups and downs, however, so it is only good if you want to invest for ten years or more. When you invest in hot tips or fads, you are gambling. You could lose as easily as gain.

Money can beget money, and its offspring
can beget more, and so on.
Five shillings turned to six....and so on
till it becomes a hundred pounds.

BENJAMIN FRANKLIN

**Law #3:
Put your money
to work for you.**

"The rich man in the original *The Richest Man in Babylon* was a money lender, and the only examples of how to put your money to work were based on lending. Today, this is not practical for most people. In fact, it can even be illegal to lend people money without a license if you receive high interest rates.

"How you use your savings to work for you depends on your interests, your opportunities, and your creativity. I'll make a few suggestions here, but only *you* know what is right for you. You'll have to think hard and experiment to find the money-making opportunities that fit your abilities and interests.

*How can you
make your
savings work
for you?*

"A big area of investment is rental properties. It's also possible to own and lease many types of equipment for farms and businesses.

*Start a
business.*

"Starting your own part-time business is another way to invest both your money and your time. Maybe you can buy and sell items on eBay. Or start a part-time business that you can do evenings and weekends.

"I've known people who bought used cars, fixed them up, and resold them for a profit.

"You may be able to invest in collectibles like art, coins, stamps, books, or some other item you are knowledgeable about. But watch out for fads.

"If you know people who own businesses, you may be able to invest as a silent partner. Or, like the original rich man of Babylon, you may find a safe way to lend money to people you trust.

"If your children will be going to college, investing money in a college account may save you from future price increases, and could earn

Be creative.

tax-free interest. Most states and schools have programs you can investigate.

"If you're a professional, you may be able to invest in self-publishing a booklet, or a book. This could provide you direct profits from sales, as well as consulting work or promotions in your job.

"All forms of investments have risks. If you make a mistake, learn from it and move on. When

**Accept
risk.**

you find the right way to put your money to work, you are on the path to building a stream of wealth."

Protect Yourself Against Loss

Law #4

"When you have extra money, you will be sorely tempted to spend it or to invest in schemes.

"Not losing what you have is a key to building wealth. Don't be misled by your own desire to

**Law #4:
Seek safety in
your investments,
and the advice of
the successful.**

make money fast. And be especially careful of other people who try to help you invest your money. The advice of people who do not regularly make money is usually worthless."

Make Your Home a Profitable Investment

Law #5

"If you're saving 10 percent of your income and spending 90 percent, any part of the 90 percent that you can turn to investment is an extra advantage," said Bob. "If you rent, you're making profits for your landlord. Plus, you're not enjoying the pleasure of controlling your own space. There's something special about having your own yard, and the ability to do what you want in it without permission.

**Law #5:
Own your own
home.**

"In many areas, the cost of owning a house is little more than the cost of renting. In other areas, payments on a house are more than the cost of renting. Until you save enough for a normal down payment, lease-to-own or low down-payment opportunities do exist.

"If you stay in your house, in most areas, over the long term, it will go up in value. It can become your biggest asset.

"Your interest payments are tax deductible. In addition, the tax laws in the US have changed so that you can sell your primary residence every

**Real estate can
work.**

two years and keep all the profits you make, tax free, up to $500,000 for a married couple. If you live in an area with appreciating houses and don't mind fix-up work and moving, this is a tremendous source of tax-free income.

"If you own a house but plan to sell it in the next few years, putting money into upgrades in the kitchen will let you enjoy fancy appliances now, and you'll often receive more than you invested when you sell your house.

"If you have a mortgage on your house and plan to stay in it for many years, you can make extra payments on the principle. By paying off $100 in extra principle each month, your return on that investment can be high, since you're not paying interest on the same money over and over."

Plan for Your Retirement

Law #6

"Setting aside money in a retirement plan, such as a 401(k), is wise in two ways. You ensure that there's money for the future, and you 'grow' that money without paying taxes—you only pay taxes on it when you withdraw it.

"Life insurance and a will provide for your family if you or your spouse dies. 'Term' insurance is fine for a death benefit. 'Whole life' can be a valuable source of guaranteed savings as well.

Law #6:
Provide for your old age, your health, and the protection of your family.

"Health insurance or an HMO insures you against today's very high medical costs. Three days in the hospital can cost you a year's salary these days!"

Give me a stock clerk with a goal,
and I will give you a man who
will make history. Give me a man without
a goal, and I will give you a stock clerk.

J.C. PENNEY

* * *

The man who does not read good books
has no advantage over the man
who cannot read them.

MARK TWAIN

Law #7

Increase Your Earning Potential

"Your most valuable asset is your knowledge. Many people with 20 years of experience on the job actually have only one year of experience repeated 20 times! If you want to earn more, you need to increase your knowledge and your skills.

"If you work for others, talk to your boss about opportunities available and skills needed. A smart boss always trains his replacement so *he* can be promoted!

"If your current job setting doesn't value your new skills, usually another one will. Investing in yourself will put you ahead of your peers. In one informal survey, fewer than 5 percent of professionals invested more than $100 a year in training courses. Most spent far more on the *outsides* of their heads, getting haircuts, than they did on the insides!

> **Law #7:**
> **Cultivate your own powers. Increasing your knowledge and skills increases your options and earning power.**

"If you work for yourself, then you know what training you need to enable you to serve clients better or capture new and interesting work."

CONCLUSION

"You have now heard the seven laws of money," said Bob. "They may sound simple, but if you apply them rigorously, you will be better off.

"Wealth is not a single animal that all men must chase and only one may catch. Wealth grows for all as more people apply the principles of wealth. As all produce more, all can enjoy more.

"It's your job to apply these rules to your own lives and then go forth and teach them to others so we can all enjoy increased prosperity despite the ups and downs of normal economic cycles."

You can learn about the laws of wealth.

4

Seven Keys
to Financial Success

A heavy purse makes a light heart.
16TH-CENTURY ENGLISH PROVERB

*T*he class for the mayors' group resumed the next week.

Bob Kozlowski, the most successful businessperson in town and the leader of the class, opened with, "If you could have $10,000 *or* a book telling you how to get ahead, which would you take?"

"The $10,000," chorused the class.

"And what would you do with the $10,000?"

"Take a vacation."

"Buy jewelry."

"Buy an RV."

"Go to Las Vegas."

These were some of the answers shouted out.

"So the money would be gone and you'd have either nothing to show for it or an asset like a car that depreciates quickly," said Bob. "I'm not saying that the memories from a trip aren't worth-

Don't spend quickly.

while, but until you have financial security, every dollar you spend now is $10 you could have had later if you'd invested it properly. I strongly recommend that you delay gratification, save and invest now, and reap the rewards later."

Knowledge Brings Money

"In fact," said Bob, "you'd be better off with the wisdom of these lessons than you would be

Training children about money.

with a quickly squandered $10,000.

"I have an example of that in my own family," said Bob. "When my children were quite young, I sat them down and told them that the children of the rich usually turn out to be both un-happy and unskilled in making and managing money. Often they have no career goals, are spoiled by their parents,

and know they'll inherit money no matter what they do.

"I told each of them that I wouldn't be spoiling them and that I might give all my money to charity. To inherit anything from me, they'd first have to prove that they could make money themselves and earn respect from the world.

"However, I did tell them that I would pay for college—just tuition, fees, and room and board. And if they graduated from college or decided to start their own businesses, I would give them some advice and a small financial stake.

"So, what happened? One went to work for a big company, and one became a social worker. My third didn't like school. He decided to start his own business instead.

"True to my word, I sat each one down to impart my 'wisdom' and I gave them each $50,000 as a stake.

"Like the $10,000 example at the beginning, the $50,000 was enough to make them careless, but not enough to support them for long.

"I was interested to see how they handled the money, but my advice could be worth more to them than the money if they used it. I organized it into seven keys."

THE SEVEN KEYS TO MONEY

Key #1 → Money Comes to Those Who First Save 10% of Their Income

"Of course, I repeat this law over and over. It's the foundation of all of your dealings with money. In addition to the value of invested savings, putting aside 10 percent does three other things for you.

"First, it makes you more confident. You don't worry about little money emergencies. You build pride in your own self-control. Second, having money allows you to take advantage of opportunities. And your confidence will tend to attract more opportunities.

"Third, you start creating an estate. This gives your family security now. And it gives you some retirement security later."

Key #2 → Learn Before You Earn

"If you have no knowledge of money and investing, you will be afraid of both. There are many fine books about all aspects of money and investing. Like the famous self-help-book author, Og Mandingo, you can start your education at the library. These discussions give you plenty to go on, but there are many other tapes, classes, and people who can help you as well."

Key #3 **Be a Positive Thinker**

"Anyone can find problems with *any* course of action. But negative thinking is not constructive for you or the type of successful people you want to be around. The *doer* focuses on the upside. If you never take action, you'll never gain success—or the experience needed for success. Many times, the worst that can happen if you don't succeed is a minor setback that you learn from.

"Obviously, this doesn't mean that you plunge ahead blindly. You prepare yourself. You obtain the best advice possible. You anticipate the problems. But then you must commit yourself in order to gain the benefits. Too many people let their negative thoughts scare them away from areas they can succeed in. They never even get started."

*Any fact facing us is not as important
as our attitude toward it,
for that determines our success or failure.*

NORMAN VINCENT PEALE

Invest in Areas You Are Passionate About

"Nothing supports success like passion! If you love what you do, your passion will carry you past the rough spots. Very few of us can make a success of something that we really don't care about. If I told you that I would get you into medical school and pay your tuition, would you want to study anatomy, chemistry, and so on for years just to make a lot of money later on? Most people wouldn't want to do the work of medical school. Or, at the other end of the status scale, panhandlers can make as much as $40 an hour. That's far more than the average wage in this country. Would you want to be one?

"There are hundreds of things most of us *could* do. Invest your time and money in the ones that you really *care* about."

If It Seems Too Good to Be True, It Probably Is

"You'll lose money if you invest in long shots, or if you expect to receive very high returns. You'll sometimes invest wildly because you

*A journey of 1,000 miles begins
with the first step.*

CHINESE PROVERB

are unrealistic. Other times, scam artists and crooks will be after your money.

"Playing commodities markets is a good example. Unlike the stock market, in commodities there is a loser for every winner. And you're 'playing' against the producers and users of the commodities who have more information than you'll ever have. Day-trading stocks is another gamble."

Key #6   To Make Progress, You Have to Get Started

"Many people have good ideas or intentions, but few take action. Don't be afraid to commit yourself. Even if your start is just reading in the library, *you must take action to get results.*

"Action makes things happen for you. The more action you take, the more you'll learn to take smarter action next time. You will often learn more from your mistakes than from your successes. This is how we gain experience."

Key #7   Build Your Own Habits

"Once you've found actions that work, turn them into habits. By creating a habit, routine ac-

Success seems to be connected with action.
Successful people keep moving.
They make mistakes, but they don't quit.

CONRAD HILTON

tions become easier and you are freed up for more creative activities. Habits also make it easier for you to continue to take action even when you don't feel like it or if you hit some other barrier."

SUMMARY

"In our discussions, I've covered many rules that will help you start and grow your fortune. These seven keys to success are useful to build into your thinking and your actions now. Save money to build a stake; learn before you earn; be a positive thinker; invest in areas you're passionate about; if it seems too good to be true, it probably is; commit to action; and build successful habits."

Take positive action to get ahead.

WHAT HAPPENED TO BOB'S KIDS?

"Some of you will be curious about how this advice worked out in my own family," said Bob.

The Cautious One

"My child who went to college and became a social worker put his $50,000 in the bank and collected interest. From a financial point of view, my social worker showed that he would not be the one to inherit and use my estate. As mentioned earlier, leaving your money in the bank is equivalent to the old Bible story of the person who buried his talents (money) for safekeeping. Money that doesn't 'work' is wasted.

"However, by not squandering the money, my social worker had at least demonstrated caution and prudence. And by working in his field for years, he demonstrated passion and commitment. In my estate, I expect to set up my own foundation and offer this son a chance to head it or serve on the board to decide where the money is given away."

The Go-Getter

"My daughter, who graduated from college and got a job in a big company, gained experience but decided she didn't particularly like corporate bureaucracy. After five years, she started her own consulting firm. She is already doing well, building on her contacts from the corporate world. She invested some of her $50,000 in her new business, and already has 12 employees.

"She has demonstrated that she can take initiative and responsiblity—she's the kind of person who should inherit my fortune. Rather than taking over my company, it will probably be sold with the money going to her. Then it will be her turn to train and test the next generation for their money competence."

The Unfocused Entrepreneur

"My oldest boy didn't like school and went directly into his own business. He lost his $50,000 in a risky investment.

"His business did well for a while, and he made a lot of money. By age 21, he was living high, driving a Porsche, and living in a big house. Then he lost interest and sold his business.

"He thought he could make anything succeed, but his next business struggled. Then he built a 'spec' house for resale in an expensive market. He was spending money without any income for two years. He barely scraped out of that hole.

"Unfortunately, he wouldn't focus his talents on a single, profitable business. He dabbled and dawdled, still living fairly high. He lacked focus, and waited for inspiration to strike.

"Fortunately, he is a charmer and married money. He won't inherit any of my fortune but perhaps someday he'll find something that holds his attention and focuses his energies."

They who provide much wealth for
their children but neglect to
improve them in virtue,
do like those who feed their horses high,
but never train them to be useful.

SOCRATES

5

How to Make Your Own Luck

Good luck can be enticed by accepting opportunity.
GEORGE S. CLASON

*E*verybody has times when, with just a little better break, they would have received that promotion, made more money, or even married their high school sweetheart.

After Bob's lectures to the mayors' group, John and Roberto stopped by to chat about the issue of luck.

"Bob, I was wondering what role you thought luck had played in your great success," said John.

"I've had good luck in many different ways. I had the good luck to be born in the richest country in the world, to have had some good teachers, to have been around during the computer revolution, and so on."

What Is Luck? ❄

"To answer your question, you have to define luck. The classic definition is blind chance, a total accident that happens to you for no reason.

"Some believe that luck comes from God. Others have more 'New Age' beliefs that luck is a matter of positive thinking—if you put out good vibrations, they tend to come back to you. The saying 'what goes around, comes around' reflects this.

"Gambling is the purest case where luck can be observed. It is exciting to win occasionally, but the laws of probability say that in the long term the house will win and you will lose. Even if heads come up ten times in a row, blind chance is still determining the outcome of each toss.

Easy money doesn't stick.

"Some people win at gambling. But do you know anyone who obtained money that way who used it as the basis for a fortune? Research shows that not only do such 'winners' not build fortunes, but within a few years most lottery winners, and even people who inherit money, end up back where they started. Money obtained without effort seldom changes your life.

<table>
<tr><td>

**The active
definition of
luck.**

</td><td>

"I like to define luck as preparation meeting opportunity. The things *you* do to prepare yourself and to go looking for opportunities

</td></tr>
</table>

will bring you more luck. Exactly *which* opportunities you find may be based on blind chance. Through the years, many people have commented about the relationship between hard work and luck. People who are consistently 'lucky' in business seem to be the ones who work the hardest—both in preparation and in looking for opportunities.

"We all are exposed to opportunities, but most people don't act on them. Or they don't prepare themselves or put themselves in situations where they can meet extra opportunities. It is their own shortcomings that cause them not to be lucky."

Procrastination Kills Luck and Wealth

"That sounds like us," said John. "For many years we drifted along. We wouldn't have known opportunity if it had bitten us!"

The harder I work, the luckier I get.
SAMUEL GOLDWYN

* * *

Diligence is the mother of good luck.
BENJAMIN FRANKLIN

"But since coming to you," said Roberto, "our luck has gradually changed for the better. But, I guess that's not really luck. We've been following your advice."

"Just so," said Bob. "There's never a perfect time to save money and invest, but you must start anyway. That puts you on the path to making your own luck and building an estate.

"If you procrastinate, you are rejecting opportunity. When you feel that an opportunity is a good one, act promptly.

"You can always talk yourself out of action if you want to. Instead, train yourself to *take action*. If you make a few small mistakes, it is your tuition in the school of making your own luck."

Don't fail from inaction.

Roberto said, "When I think about the past, it is my mistakes through *inaction* that I regret the most. Whether it was the time that I was too afraid to ask a beautiful girl for a date or the time I didn't invest in a friend's business. *Those* are the mistakes I regret."

Success is 99 percent failure.

SOICHIRO HONDA

* * *

Success is going from failure to failure
without loss of enthusiasm.

WINSTON CHURCHILL

* * *

If you want to succeed,
double your failure rate.

THOMAS WATSON

Failure Leads to Success

"You should never be afraid to make mistakes," said Bob. "You know the old riddle about achieving success? You find success by gaining experience. And you gain experience by making mistakes. So without failures, there is no success! This is true of most entrepreneurs, including me. Most who achieve big successes have had multiple failures. But they didn't let those stop them; they learned from them.

"Most people hope that 'good luck' will *find them* without any effort on their part. They may have never thought about taking action. Or they may have been afraid of failure. Or they may have fallen into the bad habit of procrastination and missed their opportunities."

CONCLUSION

"You must work on yourself to create your own 'luck.' First, increase your skills to better take advantage of opportunities. Second, get out in the world so that you will be exposed to more opportunities. Third, learn to take prompt action when such opportunities present themselves."

Luck Doesn't Just Happen

"If you stay at your desk, or in your office, you will only find limited opportunities. Instead, if you call people, make contacts online, and network in groups, you are much more likely to meet people and the opportunities they bring."

Luck is preparation meeting opportunity.
Luck comes to people of action.

6

The Dangers of
Lending Money

*If you lend money, you make a secret enemy;
if you refuse, an open one.*
VOLTAIRE

A few months after their discussion about
making your own luck, John and Roberto made
an appointment with Bob.

"We enjoyed your lectures a few months
ago," said Roberto. "Thanks again for inviting us
to sit in. Your talks reminded us of some things
and covered a few different perspectives and new
points. The questions we answered for people
probably didn't contribute much."

"It was valuable for them to hear from two
'regular guys.' It's important that they see someone besides me who is succeeding," said Bob
smiling. "You also gave them someone to ask
questions of *about me* during the breaks!"

A "Problem" of Success

"Your earlier coaching has paid off!" Roberto exclaimed. "Now I have a new problem. It's a problem that may come with success. One of my deals paid off quicker and bigger than I expected. I don't have anything planned for the money immediately except to put it in the bank. So now my family and friends are after me to let them share in my 'windfall' in various ways."

"That's normal enough," said Bob. "When people we know get money suddenly, we often feel that they should share their good fortune. Surely you have the willpower to just say no."

"Sure, it's easy to say no to most people, but how can I refuse my own sister whom I love?"

"But your sister should feel loyalty to you too, so she shouldn't want to deprive you of the benefits of your efforts!"

"It's not for her personally. It's her husband. She's sure that, with a loan from me, he can set up his own professional practice and be very successful. Then he can repay me from his profits."

Others Expect Things of Those with Money

"Roberto," resumed Bob, "this is an important topic. Money brings with it responsibilities, and it changes you in the eyes of other people. It puts you in situations where your good intentions may cause problems.

"There's more to lending money than simply giving it to people. When I was a kid, I read a book called *Mr. Wilmer,* about a man who could talk to animals. After Mr. Wilmer discovered that he could talk with the animals, he used to enjoy spending time at the zoo and other places where he could overhear the animals talking to each other."

Helping Others Can Backfire

"One night, Mr. Wilmer heard a horse that pulled a tourist buggy complain to another horse: 'I have to pull this buggy all over town, while you're retired to the stables for stud.' The second horse was sympathetic and said, 'If you want to have a day off, all you have to do when they come

The holy passion of Friendship will
last through a whole lifetime—
if not asked to lend money.
MARK TWAIN

to harness you in the morning is lie down and bel-
low. They'll decide you're sick and give you the
day off.' The first horse took the advice and got
out of working. However, the stables harnessed
up the retired horse instead. So, while he'd only
intended to help his friend, he
ended up doing a hard day's
work that he wasn't used to.

"That night, Mr. Wilmer
listened to their exchange. The
first horse said 'Thank you, friend.
Because of your advice, I enjoyed a day off.' The
second horse replied, 'And I am like any other
simpleminded fool who starts out to help a friend
and ends up doing his work for him. From now on,
do your own work. And I overheard the owner say
that if you were sick any longer, he'd send you to
the glue factory.'

"After that, their friendship ended. Can you
see the moral of the story, Roberto?"

"I suppose it's to not take on the responsibilities of my friends and family. And I don't want
to. Yet I want to help, too. Don't you think loans
to family are safe?"

Loans to Family Are Dangerous

"You got the moral," said Bob. "As for the 'safety' of lending money to friends and family, first a borrower has to believe that it is *your* money and you deserve it. Family and friends always seem to feel at some level that you should share with them if you are better off, so in their minds, it can become *their* money!

"A safe loan lets the borrower make money so that he can repay you, and it is structured so that he *wants* to repay you. If the borrower doesn't repay, you should have collateral. Yet, would you take your sister's house if the loan wasn't repaid?"

"No, I wouldn't be able to do that," said Roberto.

"I've found that with loans to family and friends, you are better off making them a gift of the money. If you don't expect to get your money back, you won't be disappointed. Instead of a dunning force that they come to hate, you become the most generous person they know."

Don't Lend to Unqualified Borrowers

"Your brother-in-law also falls into another dangerous category to do business with: the inexperienced business person. If he had a strong knack for business, he'd probably already have saved money or found a partner who had money.

"The first time a new business person does anything, he or she makes mistakes. *You* could end up paying for them. And you aren't even sure if your brother-in-law has a strong passion to start a business. *People without strong drive and passion for what they are doing seldom succeed.*

"How much does your brother-in-law know about the business he would start? Has he had experience in that business? Does he have strong contacts who would help him succeed? Has he supervised employees before?"

Many shouldn't start businesses.

"No, I don't think that he has any of those advantages," said Roberto. "But he *is* family and family is important to me."

"It would be better for him, and wiser for you, to counsel him

Neither a borrower nor a lender be.

SHAKESPEARE (HAMLET)

to find a way to start without a big investment. After all, should he fail and lose your money, if he is honorable and pays you back, it will put a burden on him for years. If he doesn't pay you back, he will resent you, and it will drive a wedge between you and your sister."

Protect What You Have

"If you keep your money and put it to work safely, Roberto, it will repay you and your family for your lifetime, and beyond, to your descendants.

"When you have something to protect, be more cautious. That's another reason your brother-in-law may not be a good borrower. If he has nothing of his own at risk, when things get tough, he may quit and go back to a regular job."

SUMMARY

"To accumulate money you have to take some risks. You can control both the risks *you* take and the efforts *you* put in to be a success. When you lend money to *others,* you can't control their risk taking *or* their efforts. Only lend to people who can use the money to make more money or to those who have good collateral.

"And remember another lesson—that every dollar you put to work now will be worth many dollars in the future. So, if you lose a dollar on a loan now, it represents far more damage to your future wealth *and* your ability to help your family.

"With wealth comes both responsibility and temptation. Taking care of what you have is often as hard as earning it in the first place."

> *Lending money has many dangers.*
> *Better a little caution than a great regret.*

7

Building Your "Walls of Babylon"

In the multitude of counsellors there is safety.
PROVERBS 11:14

"**I**n olden days," said Bob, "Babylon was protected by its massive walls. Similar walls also supported the famous Hanging Gardens of Babylon that you've heard about as one of the Seven Wonders of the Ancient World."

Modern Walls of Protection

"The great walls of Babylon represented safety. Today we have walls of safety such as health insurance, life insurance, savings, investments, and the legal system itself. As you build your fortune, you should also create *your* walls of security for your fortune and your family, John and Roberto. Because you are achieving financial success, you now need to focus more on protecting what you have."

Preparation Avoids Problems

"The fact that you have 'walls' tends to keep many possible threats from materializing. Of course, it's not enough simply to *build* walls. You should anticipate threats and dangers, and work to avoid them. For instance, you don't just have insurance for the theft of your car, you also lock the doors and don't leave your keys in the car.

"You also have to actively defend your walls when you are attacked. That means having competent advisers such as lawyers, accountants, financial planners, and insurance agents who are proactive on your behalf.

"Once you've built your defenses and your support team, don't worry if your defenses *aren't* used. For instance, you have fire insurance but you hope you will *never* have the disruption of a fire."

Your Financial Security

"Life insurance is your first line of defense if you have other people depending on you. If you are young, you may want to use term insurance. It is the cheapest insurance but accumulates no value. The cost will also go up as you get older.

"A common recommendation is to buy term life and invest the difference you save over buying whole life. However, very few people have the discipline to 'invest the difference.'

INSURANCE POLICY

Save while you protect

"Whole life is the life insurance most people are familiar with. It pays a death benefit *and* accumulates cash value. You can borrow from your policy tax free, and it can represent an asset in your estate.

"I can't give you legal and tax advice, and each state and country has different rules. In the United States, if you set up a personal S Corporation or LLC, you can buy your life insurance with pretax dollars. You can also put life insurance in other people's names to take it out of your estate or to pay taxes due when you die. Whole life and guaranteed annuities are powerful tools for your estate when used right."

The Importance of a Will

"The second line of security for your family is your will. Various statistics say that as many as 70 to 80 percent of people don't have a will. The lack of a will takes control of your estate away from you and gives it to the courts. For instance, in some states, if you are married and die without a will, half of your estate automatically goes to your spouse and the other half to your parents. Most adults would prefer other arrangements. For instance, you'll probably want to include your children, or even grandchildren, directly in your estate.

"While you should consult a lawyer, you can do a preliminary will yourself. Wills are one of the few legal documents where a handwritten document by you has clear legal status."

Retirement

"One of the increasing risks today is the problem of outliving your money. As life spans increase, and as the baby boomers age, we will have fewer and fewer young workers to support more and more long-lived retirees.

"Unlike some doomsayers, I am sure that Social Security will survive. However, you won't want to live solely on the $1,000+, even inflation adjusted, that Social Security will pay you monthly.

"Annuities are a form of insurance usually used for retirement income. They generally provide you a guaranteed income, with a possibility of higher returns if their investments do well. Annuities allow you some creative financial alternatives when properly designed and used."

Trusts and Other Structures

"I cannot give legal or tax advice. That's another reason you need to build your team of experts. The details get a little complicated. However, it's worth mentioning that there are various legal forms that can protect you in different ways.

"For instance, a living trust lets you avoid probate. This can save your heirs time and money, and provides privacy. Probate exposes your estate to public view. It also entails fixed costs to a lawyer and the court. Probate can be dragged out, and there has been considerable fraud in probate courts, where assets were sold to insiders at low prices."

Put not your trust in money,
but put your money in trust.

OLIVER WENDELL HOLMES

Health Insurance

"With health care costs escalating, you need to protect yourself and your family with some form of health insurance.

"Health costs are going up far faster than inflation. One answer has been HMOs. Of course, they're so big that waiting lists are often long for any but emergency treatment.

"If you have enough money to pay directly for simple doctor visits and checkups, one approach is to use health insurance only for catastrophic coverage. That is, your insurance only applies after you've spent an amount like $5,000. In an area this important, you'll want to consult with experts on the protective 'Walls of Babylon' that are right for you."

Self-Employment Income

"If you have self-employment income (or own your own company), there can be benefits to incorporating yourself as a Sub S, or using a limited liability corporation, often called LLCs, for similar purposes. These legal entities may allow you to put more pretax money in a defined-benefit retirement plan or life insurance. For instance, if you lend your corporation money to use for a retirement plan for you, you may end up with as much as 150 percent of your income as a retirement contribution and a tax loss as well.

"Many pension advisers don't tell you that defined-benefit plans let you put away much more for retirement than defined-contribution plans. Nor do they show you the big advantages of an individual 401(k) for the self-employed. This is another area where you need knowledgeable advisers."

Get Expert Advice

"Only some retirement accounts are safe from lawsuits and creditors. Trusts can be set up to protect your assets from the same dangers.

"The purpose of my advice to you is not to raise your worries about dangers to your wealth, but to give you forewarning so you can avoid problems as you accumulate an estate. The dangers mentioned here are simply examples of why it is valuable to have good advisers on your side, from insurance to financial planners to tax and legal experts."

Baseless Lawsuits

"When you have money, sometimes people will make you a target. There's no way you can stop people from suing you, except to keep a low profile and make it hard to get at your assets through trusts and other legal devices. Setting these up is part of preparing your 'Walls of Babylon.'"

Financial Fraud

"A threat against your financial security that is increasing fast in the 21st century is paper- or computer-based theft, including identity theft. It is hard to obtain estimates of the extent of this threat, however, banks and credit card companies in the United States alone lose billions of dollars to fraud. The US Federal Trade Commission estimated total costs to society at $53 billion per year!

"While fraud and theft can happen through the use of high tech, the most common means of stealing your identity, credit card numbers, and so on are low tech. For instance, one family recently had a "courtesy check" sent by a credit card company cashed at a local grocery store by an unknown person. The check must have been stolen out of the mailbox or recycling bin.

"What can you do to protect yourself? First, use a paper shredder or burn all old papers with your personal numbers on them. The advice that most people don't follow is to get a locking mailbox. Sign all your credit cards immediately and memorize PIN numbers rather than carry them around. By being alert to this problem, you can avoid many risks.

Your bank and computer and financial advisors can help you be safer."

CONCLUSION

"In the days of Babylon, armies actually attacked the famous walls. Today, the direct dangers from war and terrorism are slight for the average person. You need to build *your* 'Walls of Babylon' against other threats to the estate, health, and well-being of yourself and your family. By being alert to this problem you can minimize many risks."

You need to protect your assets
and your family.

8

Living Up to
Your Obligations

Character is simply habit long continued.
PLUTARCH

"You've both met my chief assistant, Sam" said Bob. What did you think of him?"

"Very professional," said John.

"He seemed to be right on top of all the details without being obtrusive," reported Roberto.

"Yes, he's very competent. He makes me more effective. And he does things the way I like them to be done. He sees his job as anticipating my needs. However, he wasn't always that way. He's a good illustration of someone who didn't contribute much, fell out of the system, and then worked his way back. He developed character only after failing."

An Irresponsible Debtor

"Sam got a job at a local company. His position required no great initiative or responsibility. He was charming and agreeable and got by okay. He was a bachelor and lived it up."

Borrowing Sinks You

"In order to keep up his lifestyle, he borrowed money from his mother. He borrowed money from friends at work. He borrowed money from his poker buddies. Every time he got his paycheck, he already owed more money than he had. He always had 'too much month' for his money.

"One day his company cut 8 percent of the employees company-wide. Everybody liked Sam, but he didn't perform any crucial job functions, so he was cut. Sam couldn't get another job.

"By now, Sam had no friends who would lend him money. He had no savings, so he lost both his apartment and car. His mother lived in another town and Sam didn't want to move back there. When his unemployment ran out, he couldn't afford the cheap room he was renting. Soon he was homeless, living on the street and in various shelters."

Up From the Bottom

"I met Sam when I gave a talk at a workshop for the homeless on how to prepare yourself for the job market. People put together simple résumés, were given donated suits, and were told about being on time and other simple job tips.

"Most of the people in the workshop were aiming at fast-food jobs or at developing simple clerical skills. Sam spoke to me about business in a broader sense. I started mentoring him casually."

Educate Yourself

"It turned out that the only constructive thing Sam had done since becoming homeless was to spend time at the library. It was warm and quiet and nobody bothered him. He'd read some classic self-improvement books, like

Debt is the slavery of the free.

PUBLILIUS SYRUS

Think and Grow Rich. He realized that his situation wasn't just bad luck. He hadn't been contributing much to the world, so nobody missed him when he lost his place in it. I recommended a few more books for him, such as *Acres of Diamonds*.

"I told Sam that one of the keys to success was to take responsibility for yourself and your actions. I pointed out to him that the money he'd borrowed belonged to others and he was depriving them of it. His mother was older and especially needed the money he'd borrowed. I told him to get a job and start paying back the people he owed, even if his payments were only a token at first."

Take Control

"I also pointed out that he had been drifting through life focused on short-term pleasures. Like most people, he hadn't spent any money on courses or books that would make him better at his job. Like many, he did what was asked of him, but took little initiative.

"I explained that the only way to get ahead was to give value to others. For instance, if he wanted to get a job, he had to deliver far more

You can't escape responsibility
for tomorrow by evading it today.

ABRAHAM LINCOLN

value than his salary to make up for the cost and risk his employer took in hiring him.

"I was blunt with Sam, and while he didn't enjoy being criticized, he took it pretty well. He'd avoided applying for jobs he considered low level, but finally he got a janitorial job cleaning an office building at night. During the day, he slept and then went to the library."

Sam Accepts Responsibility

"It took Sam six months of low-level, thoughtless work to start paying back some of the money he owed. Over the next few months, he found 17 different people who he owed money to and talked to each one. Some had forgotten the minor amounts he owed. Others remembered and were hostile.

"Over the next six months, Sam repaid many of the small debts and made token payments on the larger ones. During this period, several of the people he paid back helped him in small ways. For instance, he got short-term jobs from a couple to repay his debts to them. One of these turned into a part-time day job when he performed better than expected. This allowed him to repay even more money.

"Sam had kept in touch with me occasionally during this period. I'd given him bits of advice and watched his progress. I offered him a janitorial position with my company and told him that if he did well, he would be welcome to apply for other jobs within the company."

Contribute Where You Are

"Within a couple of months, Sam offered a few minor suggestions to improve my business. I let him work on implementing one of them in the shipping department. Soon I assigned him to deliver mail from the mailroom to the executive floors. He kept his eyes open and learned how the business was run.

"When a junior executive position opened up, I gave it to Sam on a temporary basis. He took the opportunity to do more than he was asked. He learned about all the departments that interacted with his and he cooperated well with other people to help the company. He looked at the bigger picture and became a model employee."

Sam Performs

"More importantly, Sam continued to pay off his debts. The people he'd owed liked him more because he'd paid them back—even though some had been mad at him earlier. Several of them began to mentor him and help him with business contacts.

"Eventually, I gave Sam a chance to be one of my assistants. I told him that if he treated my business like it was his own and worked hard, I'd give him stock options and he would do well financially. He performed well, got married, and now has three children."

CONCLUSION

"Sam now is a productive citizen," said Bob. He clearly creates more value than he costs me, and he serves on the boards of several charities, saves at least 10 percent of his salary, and gives 10 percent to his church. He also volunteers time in the shelter program where I found him. Instead of just 'getting by' and contributing the least possible, he enjoys being productive. Now, he's a happy man and a credit to our town."

Find a way to live up to your obligations.

9

The Lessons Applied: John's Success

What we have to learn to do, we learn by doing.
ARISTOTLE

Several years later, John and Roberto were meeting with Bob for their yearly get-together. By now, they'd become more like friends than the students and mentor that they'd started out as.

"Well Bob," said John, "This time I thought I might do the talking and show you how powerful your advice has been over the years.

"As you'll remember, Roberto and I were in bad shape financially when we came to you. Our lives were going nowhere, and we were in the hole every month. You got us started on the path to self-sufficiency, pride, and wealth. However, you gave us your advice in small pieces and it was up to us to apply it. Now I'd like to tell you how I've put your advice together over the years. My steps are a little different than yours, but they worked for me.

"Actually," continued John, "I think that organizing your wisdom into a system makes it easier to apply, and even more powerful than getting it piecemeal. In fact, I consider my six steps to be a contribution of sorts. See what you think."

Step One: The Savings Habit

"As you know," said John, "when we first came to you, I'd been working for years but was behind financially. I owed money every month on my credit cards and was making minimum payments—which meant I'd never catch up. I even owed my parents some money I'd borrowed years before.

"Your first rule—to first pay ourselves first—really changed my perspective. At first I didn't think I could save 10 percent or more, since we never had enough money. But gradually my wife and I developed pride in saving money rather than buying the latest junk. We didn't need new outfits regularly. We could enjoy eating out at simpler places that cost less. I even started cooking two nights a week to help Mary feel like *she* was eating out."

Step Two: Saving for Retirement

"Then," said John, "I realized that I had been saving some money with my company 401(k) retirement plan. I'd been having it deducted and had almost forgotten about it. I found out that I could put in more money and my company would match it. It was like free money that I was missing out on! So I raised my payroll deductions to over 10 percent. That let me get all the company matching money, plus save more myself.

"You'd told us that the stock market outperformed other investments over ten-year periods, so I put the 401(k) in a stock index fund with the lowest management fees and didn't worry about it.*

"I figured that taking the extra money out for retirement might make it harder to save 10 percent of my take-home salary. But my success in saving money for the first time gave me new confidence.

---

* For much more on 401(k)s see my book *401(k)s for Cowards* (see references on page 137).

*Pay what you owe, and you'll know
what is your own.*

BENJAMIN FRANKLIN

As it turned out, my take-home pay didn't go down the full amount because I now had less taxable income.

"It also turned out that our savings habit was strong and we could still save the full 10% of my take-home pay, plus the money Mary earned selling figurines online."

Step Three: Paying Off Debts

"Once I felt that I had some control over my money and some success in saving," said John, "your comments about paying off debts made me focus on that as an important priority. The credit-card people didn't bother me because I always paid the minimum. But their interest rates were high. I was running in place and would be paying them forever for purchases we'd long since forgotten. They were making about 15 percent interest on me. If I had been able to keep that money, it could have been working for me. Even if it was only earning 5 percent, paying the credit cards off would mean a 20 percent swing in my favor."

Time to Take Responsibility

"I felt embarrassed about the money I owed my folks," continued John. "They weren't asking for it back, but here I was a grown man, still supported by my parents in a way.

When billionaire investor John Templeton started his career, he lived on 50% of his low take-home pay! That's extreme, but it shows what can be done.

"You had said that most people can use as much as 20 percent of their income to pay off their debts. If they're saving another 10 percent, then they're living on only 70 percent of their income. Mary and I decided that we'd keep saving our 10 percent, and would commit another 10 percent to paying off our debts. I was also still putting money in my 401(k), which my company was matching.

"I knew that paying off my highest interest credit card would be the best return on my money. One of my lower-interest cards had a minimum interest charge, so for low balances it amounted to a higher rate. I paid off that card, and then started making payments on the higher-rate one."

Moving Ahead

"Even though the amount of money wasn't large, I also started sending my parents a check for $50 every month. It made me feel a lot better, and they thought of it as a surprise bonus and treated themselves to something every month 'on me.'

"After a year, our credit cards were all paid off, and we started paying my parents more. You can bet that we paid our credit-card bills every month from then on! However, I didn't move all the money to paying my parents. I increased my savings from 10 percent off the top to 15 percent and paid my parents the rest."

Step 4: Find Worthwhile Investments

"When we only had a little money saved up," said John, "there weren't too many investments we could make. In addition to Mary's eBay business, we opened a separate bank account for savings. I put some money into a plan my company has set up for employees to purchase company stock. They matched my contributions, so it was

Opportunity is missed by most people because it comes dressed in overalls and looks like work.

THOMAS EDISON

very profitable. But, I wanted to save most of the money for a better opportunity or to accumulate enough to buy a house."

Buying Your House

"After three years, I had saved enough to make a down payment on a small house, using the veterans' program with a low down payment. This raised our housing costs, but, after the tax deductions on the interest, we were close. I counted the extra costs of the house as part of my 15 percent that I was saving off the top.

"I also considered the home improvements and repairs we made to be investments. In the long term, they raised the value of the house, and we got to enjoy them along the way."

Step 5: Taking Advantage of Opportunities

"Having no debts, money in the bank, and knowing that more money was going to accumulate every month gave me new confidence.

"About once a year, an opportunity came along where I could make a few extra dollars. Once, it was a guy at work who had a chance on the weekend to paint a neighbor's house for a good profit, but he needed to buy some ladders and equipment. I made a deal with him to put up the money and work with him for half the profit. I made about $1,000 that weekend, and I sold the equipment to him over time at a profit.

"Another time, a friend's brother who owned a catering company got a big job at a local hotel and needed money to swing it. I put up the money for a truck rental and some bulk food purchases. He paid me back promptly and gave me half of what they saved by being able to purchase in bulk. It was a big profit for a two-week investment!

"My wife came up with occasional opportunities through her girlfriends. For instance, one had a chance to make several quilts for a fixed price but didn't have the money for materials.

"We avoided lending money to people. We didn't want to have friends in debt to us. We looked for short-term special situations where we could help people do something they wouldn't be able to do otherwise. We also tried to be involved personally so we could 'watch' our money."

Step 6: Being Ready to Handle Bigger Opportunities

"Our years of discipline and thinking about money as something we could control made us more confident and mature." said John. "When we inherited $150,000 from Mary's parents, we knew how to handle it.

"In the old days, we would have squandered the money on a new car, a vacation, or something else. After a year or two, we'd have been no better off.

"Because of your advice, we'd worked on finding advisors. We knew a banker, a financial planner, an insurance agent, and a stockbroker we liked. They normally only worked with clients who had a lot more money and assets than we did, but they worked with us because of the rapport we'd built with them socially.

"We used most of the money to buy both a rental property with positive cash flow and a variable annuity for retirement. We put the rest in the bank so we'd have money available for further opportunities."

SUMMARY

"I think there are other ways your advice could be organized, Bob. But these six steps worked for me: First, save ten percent off the top to invest. Second, save for retirement. Third, pay off your debts. Fourth, find worthwhile investments. Fifth, take advantage of opportunities. And, sixth, be ready for bigger opportunities.

"The heart of my progress is your advice. I think anyone who applies it can't help but be better off."

> *Organize a success system*
> *that works for YOU.*

10

Training the
Next Generation

Many receive advice; only the wise profit by it.
PUBLILIUS SYRUS

*T*he grandson of Roberto's deceased boyhood friend David had just arrived in town. Tony
was a good-looking kid. But, when he graduated
from college—in five years instead of four—Tony
didn't get a job. He'd majored in some sort of
"ology" like anthropology or sociology, but there
didn't seem to be much demand for it.

There's an old saying about families with
money: "Shirt sleeves to shirt sleeves in three
generations." This means that the first generation
starts as working class, works hard, and makes
money. But by the time their grandchildren are
done, the family is poor again. One generation
does not know how to train the next to handle
money. This was the case with Tony's family.

Life grants nothing to us mortals
without hard work.

HORACE

* * * * *

Far and away the best prize that life
offers is the chance to work hard
at something worth doing.

THEODORE ROOSEVELT

Tony's grandfather, David, had made big money, which Tony's parents inherited. But they eventually lost it all through bad investments and foolish spending.

Roberto Tries to Help

Tony's father had asked Roberto to try to give Tony a start in life and maybe improve his attitude. Tony seemed to have no appreciation for the value of money. He dressed in flashy clothes and wore too much jewelry for Roberto's taste. He acted like a bored rich kid. In memory of, and out of respect for, his friend David, Roberto had agreed to give Tony a job and show him how the world worked.

The Millionaire Next Door

Now, 20 years after he had first consulted with Bob Kozlowski, Roberto was wealthy with his own business. He'd parlayed his real estate investing into a property management business.

He wasn't "big wealthy" like Bob. He was wealthy in the way that those portrayed in *The Millionaire Next Door* are. Authors Thomas Stanley and William Danko found that the average

millionaire (usually a man) lives way under his means and runs some nonglamorous business like pest control or a body shop. He drives an older car, lives in an older house, and doesn't waste money.

Roberto's net worth was about $3 million, and he made a couple of hundred thousand a year, but he didn't spend a lot of money the way many big earners do.

"Welcome to the West Coast, Tony," said Roberto. "Take a look out the window—the whole area is really very nice. I hope you'll like it and stay."

"Why not? My grandfather made his fortune here, and I can too. As you know, my parents invested badly and ended up with nothing. They just didn't have the money-making gift of my grandfather. I don't either, but you seem to. That's why I'm happy to be able to work with you."

Non-performers Always Have Reasons

Six months later, Roberto looked out the same window to avoid looking at Tony.

"Tony, I made you my assistant so that you could see how the whole business works and get a head start. Instead, you do the minimum and act like you're doing me a favor. I want an assistant who does more than he's asked and enjoys doing it."

"Roberto, the work is boring. And you work so hard. What's the point of being rich if you don't take the time to enjoy yourself?"

Living High, Not Contributing

"What would you do to enjoy yourself if you were in my place?" asked Roberto.

"I'd live like a king. I wouldn't go to work except to pick up the checks. I'd have a garage full of fancy cars. I'd eat out at the best restaurants and have parties every night."

"Wouldn't you do any work?"

"Work is for peasants. Anyone who doesn't have to work doesn't."

Roberto thought to himself: "If the kid considers himself too good for work, no wonder there were problems."

A plan flashed into Roberto's mind. There were drawbacks to it, but he decided to act.

"Would you be interested in hearing how your grandfather and I started in life before we made our money?"

"I'd rather you just skipped to the part on how you made your money. That's all I need to know," said Tony.

Roberto's Checkered Past

Roberto ignored Tony's rude response and continued: "By the time I was your age, I'd been in a lot of trouble. Few people know that your grandfather and I were in the same gang! We weren't that bad, but we weren't that good either. For instance, you didn't have to kill someone to be initiated, you just had to beat them up. I didn't like school, so I barely finished high school. There wasn't money to go to college, anyway.

"So there I was, out of school and thinking that work was for 'losers.' With some of the other gang members, I started robbing stores and selling drugs. I had money, and time, and lots of girls."

"I never heard any of this about my grandfather! He was 'respectable.' You're not just making this up, are you, Roberto?"

"It's all true. But by the time your father married your mother, your grandfather looked like your average conservative businessman. I'm only telling you about this now to make a point. I thought it was stupid to work when I could steal. And I spent all my money on clothes, cars, and women—sort of like you're doing now."

Roberto Is Caught

"Anyway, after a couple of years I was arrested for a robbery. I hadn't actually done *that* robbery, but it was guys from my old gang who I still hung around with. It could have easily been me, since I'd pulled other robberies with them  around that time. I was held in jail for a few weeks because I couldn't post bail.

"The amazing part was that I'd never been arrested before. I was assigned a public defender. My lawyer made a deal with the DA and I went into a diversion program for first-time offenders. If I followed their rules and stayed out of trouble for two years, I wouldn't be charged and my record would be clean. I lucked out with the social worker who was assigned to me. This one happened to be fairly new on the job and still cared. She thought she could make a difference. It didn't hurt that she was young and good-looking, either!

You measure the size of the accomplishment
by the obstacles you had to overcome
to reach your goals.

BOOKER T. WASHINGTON

"I was a 'tough guy,' but she got my attention and I had to respect her sincerity. I'd had a few jobs. But I'd pretty much convinced myself that work was for suckers, so I hadn't put much effort into them. Anyway, she said that to stay out of jail I'd have to get a job. And she got me work doing cleanup for a construction company."

The Structure From Work

"The job paid well for unskilled labor, and the people there were tough enough that they weren't going to take any backtalk from me. But, they were fair. After a couple of fights, I settled down and won their respect. It was the kind of structured environment I needed in order to learn discipline.

"I'd never been that dedicated to gang life, or drugs, or crime. I'd just drifted into them because it was the easy way to go and it gave me a peer group. Most of the guys in the gang ended up in dead-end jobs where they did the minimum required, so they never advanced. Two were killed, and several spent most of their lives in jail. Your grandfather was the only one to make it big. Then, later, he moved back East.

"After I was clean for two years, they dropped the charges against me, but I kept the job. Some of the guys there were like I'd been—they didn't care much and they just drank up their pay after work every day. But most of the regulars were proud of their work, and I began to share in that pride."

Roberto Takes Initiative

"I tried to learn all the jobs on the sites, and I did more than my share. I was the first to volunteer for the 'dirty work' and the foremen appreciated it and gave me more attention and advice. I turned from a 'punk' into a top worker.

"Later I went to a community college and got a two-year degree in business. I got a job in a manufacturing plant. I worked my way up to foreman and made a fair living. Then, I sort of fell into a rut for a few years, until my friend John and I got to talking about our money problems.

"We found a mentor, Bob Kozlowski, and that's when I started to save money. Eventually, I turned part-time real estate investing into a full-time property management business. I started to make real money. And my old knowledge and contacts in construction turned out to be of value too.

"Maybe I haven't explained things very well. What I'm trying to say is that work saved me and your grandfather from wasting our lives. It was when I learned to take pride in a job well done that I began to enjoy work. Eventually, I got even more from it."

How Do You Keep the Next Generation from Becoming Spoiled?

"Look Tony, I gave you a job to get you started in life and to pass on what I've learned. But until you prove yourself, I can't really help you. I know my business isn't glamorous. It's checking buildings, making little repairs, and calling the plumber. But it's what I do, and there is more pleasure in it than you understand.

"If instead of working for me, you want to do something more exciting, like the wine business, or the music business, or the modeling business, that's fine. But you'll have to get a job in one of them and learn on your own dime.

"If you work for me the way *I* want, *and* do a good job, you can be assured of making a good living, and I'll give you options so you can own part of the business. But that would be years from now.

*Work is love made visible. And if you
cannot work with love but only with distaste,
it is better that you should leave your work
and sit at the gate of the temple and
take alms of those who work with joy.*
KAHIL GIBRAN

My mistake was probably *giving* you a job just be-cause you're the grandson of an old friend. Things that aren't earned are seldom appreciated."

Make Kids Prove Themselves

"I should have done what my mentor, Bob, did with his children. Only after they proved their ability to manage money and earn respect on their own did he give them anything else. I should have made you prove yourself before I gave you the job."

"Roberto, I'm sorry you're not happy with me, but you work all the time. What good's money if you don't have any fun?"

How to Enjoy Your Work

"As a matter of fact," said Roberto, "I enjoy my work. Sometimes I overdo it, but I get the sat-isfaction of doing something well and providing jobs for people. And your grandfather loved his business.

"Maybe what you don't understand, Tony, is the 'flow' that can come from any job. When you work at something that's involving, you lose track

Work is much more fun than fun.
NOEL COWARD

of yourself. A researcher, Mihaly Csikszentmihalyi says that you're involved and focused, but you're also relaxed. It's like being 'in the zone' for an athlete. You're not worried about how you'll do; you're too into the *process* of what you're doing."

Everyone Experiences Flow

"As I said," continued Robert, "athletes get this feeling. But you can also get it reading a book where you're so into the characters that you forget yourself. And time flies."

"I think I get that 'in the zone' feeling playing softball. I enjoy it, but it's a different kind of enjoyment," said Tony. "Kinda like I'm outside myself watching."

"Good. What I'm saying is that you should get some of that feeling from your work.

"Some people say, 'Do what you love and the money will follow.' Or 'Get the right job and you'll never work a day in your life.' It's a good thought, and if you feel passionate about owning a nightclub or something else, go for it. But you'll have to pay your dues and learn the business."

You *Can* Love What You Do

"Almost all work has the possibility of letting you experience flow as Dr. Csikszentmihalyi says, or 'getting into it' as you kids say. Lots of jobs, such as being a street sweeper, have no glamour. But you could develop pride in doing it perfectly. And you could get into the flow of sweeping. It's kind of a zen thing.

"With the right attitude, you can love your work—any work. The father of psychology, William James, roughly said that 'the motion brings on the emotion.' That is, if you *act* interested in something, you will *become* interested in it."

Pleasure from Work

"There are other enjoyments from work, like the intellectual satisfaction of a job well done," said Roberto, "or the social camaraderie of working with a group. It could even be the enjoyment of getting a big paycheck, or the pleasure of knowing that you can have a cold drink after a hot day of work.

"So, I guess I'm telling you two things, Tony. You can work in my business and learn to enjoy it. If that works out for you, you have a profitable future here.

"Or you can pursue your own passion anywhere you want. But be sure that you *do* it! Don't just drift around waiting for inspiration to strike.

"If you prove yourself somewhere and then come to me with a good business plan, I'll support you in starting your own business in whatever industry you choose. That way, you'll know you earned your credentials on your own.

"I'll respect your decision, whichever way you go. You can work for me or work somewhere else. Just be sure that you *make* a decision and *do something* well!"

> *"If you don't know where you're going, any path will take you there."*
> —The Cheshire Cat to Alice in Wonderland

"I hadn't realized you and Grandfather started in a gang! I always wanted to be like Grandfather, but I hadn't realized what he overcame. If he could succeed from there, I can too. I want to give your work a try, starting right now!"

CONCLUSION

The younger generation that has been raised with money tends to be spoiled and to look down on work. You need to help them "find themselves" and understand the pleasures of work. If your children are young, set a good example for them and encourage them to work at something.

If your kids are already spoiled, be a stern parent and make them prove themselves in life now before they waste their inheritance later.

> *Work can be a pleasure.*
> *Money acquired without effort is*
> *soon squandered.*

11

Now It's Time for *Your* Story

He who has begun is half done.
Dare to be wise; begin!
HORACE

Things may come to those who wait,
but only those things that are left
behind by those who hustle!
ABRAHAM LINCOLN

*N*ow you possess the knowledge that has helped thousands of people to get ahead financially. But the best information in the world won't help you unless you put it to use. *Now is the time for you to write the story of your future.*

You want a better life. You want to be done with money worries. You want to build security, and an estate for your family. You even want luxury.

Nothing succeeds like success.

ALEXANDRE DUMAS

10 STEPS TO FINANCIAL SUCCESS

A better life won't come from wishing. It won't come from drifting along. It won't come from a few beers after dinner and watching mindless TV shows. *It will come from new positive action on your part.* New actions will bring new results.

There is no magic wand you can wave. It will take time to create a better situation for yourself and your family. Within a year you should see real progress. It may take five years to make major changes. If you don't start now, in five years you'll still be where you are today. *So take action now!*

You can organize these ideas into your own system, or use these ten steps to get started.

1 **PAY YOURSELF FIRST.** Start putting aside at least 10 percent of your take-home income before you spend anything. Without a "stake," you will be living hand to mouth, always behind.

2 **DEVELOP A BUDGET.** If your expenses are currently too high to allow you to save 10 percent, cut your expenses. Keep track of what you spend for a month and decide if that's where you want your money to go. Also look for ways to increase your income.

3 **PAY OFF DEBTS.** Take responsibility for your debts. Pay something on them every month. Your honorable behavior will rebound to your credit. And eliminating debt will increase your financial options *and* your peace of mind.

4 **START LOOKING FOR WAYS TO PUT YOUR MONEY TO WORK.** When your money works while you sleep, you are on the way to security and wealth. Can you start a part-time business? Can you invest in safe opportunities?

5 **ACCEPT RISK, BUT BE CAREFUL.** Mistakes are learning experiences, if you take the lesson and move on. But, don't invest in schemes that are too good to be true. Lending money to family and friends is fraught with danger.

6 **DON'T PROCRASTINATE.** Be positive and action-oriented. When an opportunity comes along, seize it! Luck is preparation meeting opportunity. Get out there with your new skills and attitude and meet opportunities. Then *act* on them!

7 **INVEST IN YOUR HOME.** If you don't own a house, make that a priority. In every market there are unusual values, no-down-payment deals, lease-to-buy options, VA loans, and other ways to get started. If you do own your home, congratulations. Don't be afraid to invest in upgrading it. If you sell your house after two years, your profits from the sale are tax free. Invest them.

8 **INVEST IN YOUR RETIREMENT SAVINGS.** Many people whose companies match their contributions to 401(k) plans don't invest. Save for retirement. If you have self-employment income, create your own retirement plan.

9 **INVEST IN YOURSELF.** You must give superior value to others to be paid more. A rut is a grave with the ends not filled in. Get out of your rut and develop your skills and knowledge. You'll find people who will appreciate you more when you contribute more.

10 PREPARE YOUR "WALLS OF BABYLON."
Have a will. Have life and health insurance. Gather expert advisers for your financial matters. When you have an estate, consider a living trust to avoid probate.

SUMMARY

Now is the time to take action for a better life. We know you can do it if you'll get started. We wish you all the best. On the book's website (www.TheRichestManInBabylonForToday.com), we answer questions and offer more ideas.

> *When you follow sound financial rules and take action, good things happen.*

Suggested Readings

401(k)s for Cowards by Fred Siegel. Grammaton
    Press, 2004.

*Investing for Cowards: Proven Stock Strategies
    for Anyone Afraid of the Market* by Fred
    Siegel. Grammaton Press, 2001.

As noted in the book, the website for this book
(www.TheRichestManInBabylon.com) welcomes
your questions and has additional material.